CHUMASH

Big Buddy Books
An Imprint of Abdo Publishing
www.abdopublishing.com

Sarah Tieck

www.abdopublishing.com

Published by Abdo Publishing, a division of ABDO, PO Box 398166, Minneapolis, Minnesota 55439.
Copyright © 2015 by Abdo Consulting Group, Inc. International copyrights reserved in all countries. No part
of this book may be reproduced in any form without written permission from the publisher. Big Buddy Books™
is a trademark and logo of Abdo Publishing.

Printed in the United States of America, North Mankato, Minnesota.
102014
012015

Cover Photo: © Eyal Nahmias/Alamy; Shutterstock.com.
Interior Photos: © iStockphoto.com (p. 30); © Eyal Nahmias/Alamy (p. 29); © NativeStock.com/AngelWynn
(pp. 9, 10, 11, 13, 15, 16, 17, 19, 21, 25, 26, 27); © Mike Perry/Alamy (p. 5); Shutterstock.com (pp. 11, 23);
Wikipedia.com (p. 17).

Coordinating Series Editor: Rochelle Baltzer
Contributing Editors: Grace Hansen, Marcia Zappa
Graphic Design: Adam Craven

Library of Congress Cataloging-in-Publication Data

Tieck, Sarah, 1976-
  Chumash / Sarah Tieck.
      pages cm. -- (Native Americans)
  Audience: Ages 7-11.
  ISBN 978-1-62403-578-4
  1. Chumash Indians--Juvenile literature. I. Title.
  E99.C815T54 2015
  979.4004'9758--dc23
                          2014029806

CONTENTS

Amazing People

Hundreds of years ago, North America was mostly wild, open land. Native American tribes lived on the land. They had their own languages and customs.

The Chumash (CHOO-mash) are one Native American tribe. They are known for building ocean canoes and telling stories. Let's learn more about these Native Americans.

Did You Know?

The Chumash called themselves "the first people." Many elders say their name means "bead maker" or "seashell people."

The Chumash hold powwows to share their way of life with others. At these events, they feast, sing, and dance.

5

CHUMASH TERRITORY

Chumash homelands were in what is now southern California, near San Luis Obispo and Los Angeles. The Chumash lived along the Pacific Ocean coast and on the Channel Islands. They also lived inland as far as the San Joaquin Valley.

CHUMASH HOMELANDS

CANADA

UNITED STATES

NEVADA

UTAH

COLORADO

CALIFORNIA

ARIZONA

NEW MEXICO

MEXICO

7

HOME LIFE

Most Chumash people lived in large, dome-shaped houses. Between 40 and 50 people lived in each home. Willow branches and whalebones formed the structure. Mats made of cattails or grasses covered the roof.

Coastal homes could be 50 feet (15 m) wide. Inside, reed mats hung from the ceiling. These marked off rooms. There were platform beds with storage underneath. And, there was a fire for cooking.

The Chumash who lived farther inland built smaller homes for one family.

What They Ate

The Chumash found food in the sea and on land. They caught fish, seals, clams, and mussels. They gathered plants, mainly acorns, from the land. And they hunted deer, bears, squirrels, ducks, elks, and rabbit.

The Chumash used a mortar and pestle to ground acorns. Then, they made soup or mush.

 Fish were an important food source for coastal and island Chumash.

 The Chumash burned areas so that trees with acorns would grow better. This also brought in many deer.

Daily Life

The Chumash lived in villages. A village had homes and community buildings, including food storage. There were also sweathouses for men and women.

The Chumash didn't wear many clothes since the weather was mild. Women wore aprons. Men wore belts to carry their tools and food. Some Chumash wore headdresses or animal-skin capes.

 Chumash women wore two aprons. This included a large apron in the back and a smaller one in the front.

In a Chumash village, people had different jobs. Men hunted and fished. They were builders, artists, priests, **shamans**, and chiefs. Men spent time in sweathouses cleaning themselves. This prepared them for work, such as hunting.

The Chumash made boats to go into the ocean.

Like men, Chumash women could be chiefs, artists, or priests. Some were storytellers. They also wove baskets and ground acorns. Children learned by helping and watching others in the community.

Made by Hand

The Chumash made many objects by hand. They often used natural materials. These arts and crafts added beauty to everyday life.

Rock Paintings

The Chumash painted colorful scenes on cave walls. They painted with brushes or their fingers. They made colors from minerals.

Beads

 The Chumash made beads from olivella shells. These were used as a form of money.

Woven Baskets

 Baskets were key to Chumash life. Weavers spent a lot of time making them. Some were sealed so they wouldn't leak. Baskets held everything from babies to fish. They were covered in beautiful patterns.

Tomols

 The Chumash built large canoes called *tomols* to use in the ocean. These had flat bottoms and curved sides. Tomols often had bright colors. They could carry people or goods, such as fish.

Spirit Life

Shamans and priests were important to the Chumash religion. They led ceremonies and rituals. Priests studied the movement of the sun, moon, stars, and planets. This helped the tribe make decisions.

Chumash priests held ceremonies in caves along the coast. The winter solstice was one ritual. For this event, priests led people in dancing to honor the sun.

Chumash priests drew on the walls of caves. Some drawings can still be seen in Chumash Painted Cave State Historic Park.

19

STORYTELLERS

Stories were important to the Chumash. Some were shared around the fire for fun. Others taught people about the tribe's way of life.

The Chumash were especially known for stories about the sky. They told stories about the sun, the stars, and thunder and lightning.

Elders taught children and told them the tribe's stories.

FIGHTING FOR LAND

Long ago, Chumash villages were built along what is now the California coast. Around 1542, the Spanish began exploring the area. They were searching for gold. They came in contact with the Chumash. In 1772, the first Spanish **mission** was built on Chumash land.

Juan Rodríguez Cabrillo is remembered as the first European to explore California's coast. The Chumash met him in canoes and brought gifts.

23

By the early 1800s, thousands of Chumash lived near Spanish **missions**. Many died from sicknesses brought from Europe. They struggled as the Spanish took over their land and changed their way of life. By the late 1800s, only a few hundred Chumash were left.

Land was important to the Chumash. In 1901, the US government set up the Santa Ynez **Reservation** near their homelands in Santa Barbara. The Chumash used laws to **protect** their way of life.

Paintings show what life was like in Spanish missions.

BACK IN TIME

Before 1400

The first Chumash villages were built in Southern California.

About 1542

The Chumash met Spanish explorers for the first time.

1769

The Spanish began building missions in California. Over time, five Spanish missions were built on Chumash land.

1880

After more than 100 years of sickness, the Chumash population was about 300. In 1770, there had been up to 22,000 Chumash.

1965

The last native speaker of a Chumash language died.

1901

The Santa Ynez Reservation was set up on December 27.

THE CHUMASH TODAY

The Chumash have a long, rich history. They are remembered for their strong boats and colorful paintings.

Chumash roots run deep. Today, the people have kept alive those special things that make them Chumash. Even though times have changed, many people carry the traditions, stories, and memories of the past into the present.

Did You Know?

Today, there are about 5,000 Chumash people. Most live in California.

In 2013, dancing was a part of the inter-tribal powwow at the Santa Ynez Reservation.

29

The Chumash share creation stories. One myth says that long ago, the tribe lived on an island. The Mother Earth Spirit built a rainbow bridge for them to cross to get to new land. While crossing, some people fell into the ocean. They were changed into dolphins. So today, the Chumash call the dolphins their brothers.

GLOSSARY

ceremony a formal event on a special occasion.

custom a practice that has been around a long time and is common to a group or a place.

mission a place where religious work is done.

protect (pruh-TEHKT) to guard against harm or danger.

reservation (reh-zuhr-VAY-shuhn) a piece of land set aside by the government for Native Americans to live on.

ritual (RIH-chuh-wuhl) a formal act or set of acts that is repeated.

shaman a person who is believed to be able to use magic to heal sickness or see the future.

solstice one of two times during the year when the sun is farthest north or south of the equator.

tradition (truh-DIH-shuhn) a belief, a custom, or a story handed down from older people to younger people.

WEBSITES

To learn more about Native Americans, visit **booklinks.abdopublishing.com**. These links are routinely monitored and updated to provide the most current information available.

INDEX